WHAT YOU SHOULD KNOW ABOUT ANGELS

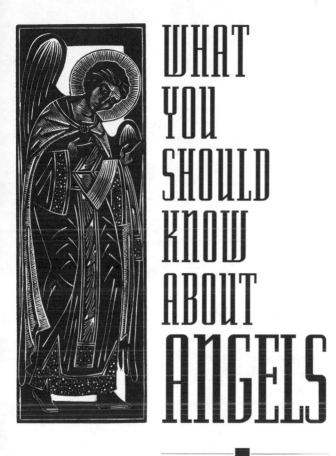

WHAT YOU SHOULD KNOW ABOUT ANGELS

Charlene Altemose, MSC

Liguori
ONE LIGUORI DRIVE
LIGUORI MO 63057-9999

Imprimi Potest:
James Shea, C.SS.R.
Provincial, St. Louis Province
The Redemptorists

Imprimatur:
+ Paul Zipfel, V.G.
Auxiliary Bishop, Archdiocese of St. Louis

Library of Congress Cataloging-in-Publication Data
Altemose, Charlene.
    What You Should Know About Angels / Charlene Altemose.
        p   cm.
    ISBN 0-89243-906-8
    1. Angels. 2. Angels—History of doctrines. 3. Catholic Church—Doctrines. I. Title.
BT966.2.a.48 1996
235'.3—dc20   95-40228

Copyright © 1996, Charlene Altemose, MSC
Printed in the United States of America
99 00 01 02 03   7 6 5 4 3

To order, call 1-800-325-9521.
http://www.liguori.org

Cover design interior art by Chris Sharp

Contents

Acknowledgments and Special Thanks

Lovingly dedicated to all the "angels" in my life:
my angelic mom, family, and friends,
especially my MSC Sisters
whose love and concern supported me
in this project
I also thank my editor, Kass Dotterweich,
for her "angelic" patience and guidance.

Introduction

A ngel. Just saying the word gives us a warm, fuzzy, good-all-over feeling; its pleasing sound elicits a sense of serenity, goodness, and integrity. Linguists classify "angel" as one of our language's beautiful words.

Although angels belong to the world we cannot see, they have been known by civilizations and cultures for thousands of years. Today polls indicate that most people believe in angels. For many, this belief stems from Christianity, Judaism, or Islam, all of which include angels in their tenets of faith. Others base their convictions on philosophic inquiry or personal communication with these heavenly beings.

These numinous beings intrigue us because we know so little about them. Theologians debate their nature; psychologists analyze them; philosophers probe the rationale for their existence; musicians and lyricists emulate their celestial harmony; artists depict them in varied shapes and forms; persons of faith testify to experiencing the presence of angels.

No longer restricted to the confines of heaven, cathedrals, or museum niches, angels are "in." Gift shops are awash with angels of every imagining, displayed in an array of marketable products: T-shirts, earrings, planters, pendants, banners, greeting cards.

People freely discuss angels on television programs, radio talk shows, and at angel seminars. While the media bring angels into our living rooms, bookstores devote entire sections to works that recount the experiences of those who have had personal angel encounters.

That angels possess a magnetic appeal is beyond question. But what makes these beings so fascinating? Why this sudden and ongoing interest in angels when the world seems so estranged from spiritual values?

Could it be that we innately crave the beautiful, the noble, the innocent? Are we becoming more attuned to the spiritual world? Do angels promise hope for a better future? Or are angels simply another fad that merchants see as a commercial asset?

Whatever the reason for this current angel phenomenon, we do know that angels bring comfort and peace. "My greatest satisfaction comes from the serenity on people's faces after they browse among all my angels," notes an angel gift shop owner.

Perhaps the present attraction is not to angels themselves but to an awareness of our human hungers that cry out for something that can bring solace to a violent and crime-infested world.

So why publish another book on angels when there seems to be "angel overload" already? The current angel trend is an opportunity to learn—perhaps discover—the role angels play in our faith life.

Angels are not newcomers on the Catholic scene; they have been part of the Church's faith life from early times. Too often, however, angels have been taken for granted. This work gives angels their due, within the parameters of faith, and provides a balanced perspective. Angels, like the saints, are honored not adored.

You are invited on a journey of faith that will delve more deeply into the angelic world. This is not a comprehensive study but a glimpse of mystery—the mystery of angels. We will explore four areas that inform and inspire us toward a more familiar rapport with angels: revelation and faith; study and speculation; human imagination and creativity; personal experience and prayer.

Part I considers the role faith plays in our understanding of angels. We scan through the Bible, the basic source of our knowledge of angels, and glimpse the angels' nature and mission. Part I also includes a summary of the Church's dogmatic teachings on angels.

Part II presents additional insights about the angelic realm through the inquiries and speculations of the Church Fathers, theologians, and other sources in Church tradition.

Part III reviews the role culture has played in nurturing our imagination with regard to angels. This part looks at how our understanding of angels has been influenced by the contributions of artists, writers, musicians, and philosophers.

Part IV cites mystics and saints who experienced and communicated with angels. It provides practical guidelines for making angels more present through deeper awareness and devotion. It also discusses the present phenomenon of angel encounters, in which people attribute extraordinary happenings to angels.

No matter how much we probe their nature, angels will remain a mystery of faith—and this may be the key to their popularity. We are always curious about that which we do not know. By delving deeply into the mystique of their world, may we become more aware of the spiritual realm and heed the angels' influence in our lives. Through these pages may your life's journey become "angel-friendly." May you realize that you do not walk alone, "for [the Lord] will command his angels concerning you / to guard you in all your ways" (Psalm 91:11). By kindling a more cordial relationship with angels—and by entering into their company—may your intimacy with the Lord deepen.

PART I

Angels:
A Mystery of Faith

For he will command his angels concerning you
to guard you in all your ways.

Psalm 91:11

Before I commenced writing this work I spent much time reflecting on angels in my own faith life. This exercise provided insights in which I realized my angel spirituality developed in three distinct phases.

My introduction to angels, which I call my "faith/discovery stage," began with a familiar picture above my bed when I was a young child. It portrayed two children walking on a wobbly bridge, their welfare obviously at risk. Overhead hovered an elegant, benevolent figure with two gigantic wings, wearing a flowing white robe. I was told this was my guardian angel sent by God to watch over me day and night. I believed that because Mom and Dad said it was true.

Although I never sensibly experienced the angel or heard a voice, I believed this unseen companion was very real and never left my side. Each evening after I said my "Angel of God" prayer, I asked, "Angel, did I make you happy today?" My angel was a presence and symbol of the spiritual world which was yet unknown to me.

I didn't question, but I had curious "wonderings" about my heavenly companion. Did my angel ever get bored watching me all the time? Did my angel ever go on vacation to heaven? Was I my angel's first charge or did my angel watch over someone else years ago? Did the angel's white robe ever get dirty? The one thing I did not question, however, was the existence of my angel. I never once feared that my angel might go away or cease to exist; belief in my angel was as sure as my faith in God.

The second phase, my "inquiry stage," began when I was a theology student and met up with Thomas Aquinas and his speculations. Although I couldn't totally resonate with the intricacies of angelic nature that scholars debated, my faith took on a deeper dimension.

Later, as a dogmatic theology professor, I was often confronted with "greater than life" questions, questions that I had raised myself in my student days. By this time I had come to realize that not every question has an

Developing an Angel Spirituality

answer, not every mystery of faith will be completely known. I satisfied my students' theological quibblings with a standard reply: "We must be content to live with an element of mystery." After many years of study and research, I still find myself discovering new insights about the ways of the Lord known only through faith.

I label the third phase in my angelic understanding as the "commitment stage." A traumatic event helped me experience firsthand the angels' protection.

It was semester registration at the college where I was teaching and several of our Sister students were going to the college to select their classes. I had planned to go along, but just as I was about to leave, I suddenly made a last-minute decision not to go. As the Sisters were returning home that afternoon, their car hydroplaned into a river. Both Sisters were sitting in the front seat and were not seriously hurt. Anyone sitting in the back seat, however, would have been crushed to death. Imagine my numb feeling when I realized how close one of us came to being a statistic. Why I stayed home that day, I do not know. To this day it remains one of my life's enigmas.

Whether or not my guardian angel actively intervened in my last-minute decision, I cannot say. But I do know that since then, my angel has been more than an imposing figure in a picture frame, more than the subject of theological inquiry. My angel has been a constant presence, an active companion along life's way, guarding and protecting me. I never begin an errand without acknowledging the nearness of my guardian companion. That experience was my "conversion" to a sincere belief in angels and a commitment to include my angel in all my life's endeavors.

Phases of Development: A Summary

As I reflect on how my understanding of angels developed, I see a striking parallel to the way the Church's understanding of angels has evolved. As a framework for this book I compare the three stages of my angel awareness to the Church's teachings on angels.

The faith/discovery stage: The Church has taught the existence of angels from God's Word and has articulated the fundamental beliefs in creed and dogma.

The inquiry stage: The Church's understanding of angels has been deepened and broadened by the writings and research of scholars and theologians.

The commitment stage: The Church has consistently encouraged devotion to angels in personal spirituality. Today many people witness to the presence of angels in their lives.

Faith Foundation for Belief in Angels

Before we explore the realm of the angels, it is helpful to consider how our faith perspective influences our belief in angels. It is impossible for us to believe in angels except through the God-given gift of faith. Ordinarily we develop faith through what we are taught within a religion or value system.

For some of us, faith is part of our heritage and legacy. For others faith comes later, after searching and discernment. Regardless of how it has evolved, faith, like all other living realities, follows a certain pattern of growth.

The existence of angels is a truth included in the Catholic's "faith-package." We respond to this belief, however, in unique ways, depending on our faith experience. Perhaps angels have been part of your faith heritage, but you never took their presence seriously, or you took them for granted, without any further thought. Perhaps angels have been intimate companions in your spiritual journey, and you've never doubted or questioned the fact. Perhaps you've accepted the general tenets of faith, but you've remained skeptical. Perhaps you've denied angels as part of any genuine faith experience.

Faith challenges us and requires our cooperation with

God's grace. There is so much about the world of the spirit we would like to know, but God reveals only that which is necessary and useful for our journey in this life. The Catholic faith helps us discover those dimensions that link us to God.

But not everything we learn as faith makes sense or can be understood. If we are to achieve a maturity in our faith, we will invariably ask "Why?" somewhere along the line. Authentic faith allows room for that doubt and those questions, and angels provide just such an opportunity to doubt and question. After all, we can speculate and wonder about angels, but we cannot scientifically prove that they exist. Angels are beyond the scope of any scientific investigation. Perhaps we will experience the presence of angels and feel at one with them as we continue this simple investigation.

Wherever we are on our faith journey or whatever stance we assume, there is no doubt that angels belong to the realm of mystery. Angels exceed human comprehension and their mystery is disclosed only through God's revelation and our response to grace.

Angels in Scripture

In faith, let us set out on our journey into the mystery of angels. We begin where God began: in the Sacred Word.

Because angels belong to the spiritual world, we could not know about them were it not for God's revelation in Scripture. When we look there, it is obvious that angels were a vital part of God's designs. God created angelic spirits to communicate the divine plan to humans. We may be surprised at how much we can know about the function and mission of angels from this fact alone.

Consider the impressive role angels played in the Bible as they burst into the earthly sphere and mediated God's plan in history. Angels crisscrossed the sacred text with swiftness and alacrity as they directed and guided human affairs.

In this chapter we walk through Scripture and observe

18

angels as agents of God's plan. If we consider the more than three hundred times angels are mentioned in the Bible, we can learn much about their mission and function. How the angels carry out the will of God is demonstrated in the many angel visitations, chance encounters, and blessed marvels they performed.

As we review Scripture, we will see angels appearing in human form, usually as young men or amiable companions. We will also read about angels who are heavenly beings wrapped in celestial splendor, shining auras, or white garments. As we hear angels sing, praise God, and convey divine messages, we will note that light, radiance, and splendor usually are associated with their mission. We will see them manifesting themselves as mere voices or as subtle but convincing beings. At other times we will see them spring onto the human stage with power, arousing awe and fear in the face of the celestial mystery.

Angels have been part of the belief system of the Hebrews from earliest times. The Hebrews believed that Yahweh engaged a company of personal "messengers," unseen but very real, who acted as emissaries from God to the Chosen People. We read of impressive works done "in the name of Yahweh."

The Hebrew Concept of Angels

The word *angel* comes from the Greek *aggelos*, which stems from the Hebrew word *mal'ak*, meaning "messenger." In the Hebrew Scriptures, these heavenly envoys actively served the purpose of God and gave God glory in a variety of activities and circumstances, appearing in the most unexpected places at the least expected times. Often, "angel" in the Hebrew Scriptures does not refer to a personal being, but is synonymous with God's word.

Because the Hebrews believed in the absolute Oneness of God, angels mentioned in the early part of the Hebrew Scriptures are closely associated with God. Remember, however, that the Hebrews were not a paper-pen people. Much of what we read today was passed on by oral

tradition from personal experiences long before it was written down. And we know how details become embellished or changed when passed on by word of mouth.

The Hebrews were more interested in the deeper meaning of events; they took no pains to analyze or describe divine interventions. For them to experience Yahweh's providence was enough, no matter what form or manner it assumed. Rather than ask "What is it?" they queried, "What does this mean?" or "What is Yahweh saying to us?" They interpreted events in the light of Yahweh's plan.

Another factor we should note as we explore the scriptural references to angels is the literary form in which these experiences were recorded. Rather than hearing the story as a literal account of a historic event, we have to look beneath and beyond, to the divine message it contains. Regardless of the form the narrative assumes, we can find the Lord on each page, in each remarkable incident involving angels.

For example, Scripture depicts some angels as intermediaries, a vital role. Remove angels from the Bible and we have a significant gap in God's divine revelations.

Throughout the story of the Hebrew nation, angels appear unexpectedly with a divine commission or message. We have no detailed information to compile a complete survey of the angelic world, but we have enough evidence in the Bible to show how God uses angels to make known the divine plan.

Note how angels assist in crucial moments as well as in minor personal dilemmas in many books of the Bible. In describing the specific occasions in the Bible in which angels appear, the present tense is purposefully applied because the stories are prototypes of how God's saving plan continues to unfold. The present verb format helps us remember God is still at work in our day.

Creation
of the Angels

One of the memorable stories that captured my childhood imagination was the graphic tale of the great war that broke out when Michael, leader of the good angels, cast Satan and his followers out of heaven. In our Bible history book, this story was placed immediately after the creation of the world and before the creation and sin of Adam and Eve. The illustration of the Archangel Michael clad in knightly armor warring with the demons made a vivid impression on my memory. Imagine my consternation when, as a serious Bible student, I discovered that the wondrous tale of the creation and fall of the angels is *not* in Genesis.

So where is the creation of the angels if it is not mentioned explicitly in the Bible? The creation and existence of angels is implied in the first verse of the first chapter of Genesis, which states that "God created the heavens...." This speculation seems plausible because in Genesis 3:24, a cherubim is standing guard when Adam and Eve are banished from Eden. The New Testament also makes several references to the fall and condemnation of Satan and the devils (2 Peter 2:4, Jude vv. 6,9 and Revelation 12:7).

So where did my Bible history get the story? It synthesized into a singular marvelous tale what is interspersed throughout Scripture concerning the creation and fall of the angels.

Angels step into Old Testament history around 1850 B.C. when Abraham extends typical nomadic hospitality to three mysterious visitors who promise Abraham he will be the father of a great nation. The exact identity of these three is not clear, but that they carry a divine message is not doubted (Genesis 18). Years later, another angel steps in—in the nick of time—to stop Abraham from sacrificing his son, Isaac (Genesis 22:11-12). Later, that same angel travels with Abraham's slave to find a wife for Isaac (Genesis 24:7).

We find other angels working on behalf of God's goodness throughout the Old Testament. For example,

Angels in the
Old Testament

two angels visit the towns of Sodom and Gomorrah. While Lot extends hospitality to them, they attempt to warn Lot to leave Sodom and Gomorrah with his family before the cities are destroyed (Genesis 19:1-22). Hagar meets a "messenger of God" in the wilderness who comforts her and provides well-water for her son, Ishmael (Genesis 16:7-12, 21:17-19).

Angels flow freely in and out of the story of Jacob. His dream of angels ascending and descending a ladder coming out of the sky has long been a popular subject of artists (Genesis 28:12). At another time an angel interprets Jacob's dream concerning the return to his own land (Genesis 31:11-13). Angels again rendezvous with Jacob at Mahanaim on his way to meet his brother, Esau (Genesis 32:1-2). Jacob's classic angel encounter occurs as he wrestles with an angel at Peniel, where his name is changed to *Israel*: "for you have striven with God and with humans, and have prevailed" (Genesis 32:24-28, Hosea 12:4). As Jacob blesses his sons at the end of his life, he prays that the angels protect them (Genesis 48:16).

While Moses primarily experiences God directly, an angel appears to him in the burning bush (Exodus 3:2). Moses is told to lead the people out of Egypt with an angel as a guide (Exodus 23:20). Like Jacob, Moses turns to the angels at the time of his death. As he recounts God's blessings at the end of his life, he calls upon the angels to glorify God (Deuteronomy 32:43).

A rather humorous event involving an angel is found in the story of Balaam and his donkey. As Balaam is on his way to curse the Israelites, an angel blocks the road and appears only to Balaam's donkey. Only when the donkey speaks does Balaam also see the heavenly roadblock and heed the angel's advice (Numbers 22:22-35).

Several biblical personalities experience God's help through the "military" intervention of angels. As Joshua approaches Jericho, for example, an angel appears as "commander of the army of the Lord" (Joshua 5:14).

Gideon, commissioned by an angel of the Lord to ward off the Midianites, skeptically asks for a sign. Acquiescing, the angel strikes the rock which ignites the flames which consume the meat and unleavened cakes that Gideon placed there (Judges 6:11-22). Angels, acting on behalf of Israel, curse the enemy and destroy them, the result being 185,000 slain Assyrians (2 Kings 19:35, 2 Chronicles 32:21, Isaiah 37:36).

Throughout the Old Testament, the prophets play a critical role in bringing the Word of God to the people. The prophets usually received their communications directly from the Lord. They, in turn, would then say to their listeners, "The word of the Lord came to me." But some prophets experienced the Lord's will through angels.

For example, Elijah, in the desert to escape from the threats of Jezebel, sits despondent and wishes to die. An angel encourages him and provides food to strengthen him (1 Kings 19:1-8). Another angel intercepts the messengers of the enemy and assures Elijah that he will not be harmed as he prophecies to King Ahaziah (2 Kings 1:3).

But angels are subject to God's commands. When God relents in his anger against Jerusalem, he orders the angels to stop the destruction: "Enough! Stay your hand" (1 Chronicles 21:15). Although Jeremiah has no communication with angels, he prays that angels accompany and guard the captives as they are led into Babylon (The Letter of Jeremiah 6:7).

Job, who experienced firsthand the power of evil, is accused of finding fault even with the angels (Job 4:18). Elihu, with tender compassion, wonders if there be an angel or mediator to ease Job of his sufferings (Job 33:23). When Isaiah receives his calling to be a prophet, he is purified through a vision of angels as they sing their three-fold praise to the Lord "Holy, holy, holy is the LORD of hosts" (Isaiah 6:3). Ezekiel, overcome with awe at visions of majesty of the Lord and the splendor of the angels, describes the overwhelming experience in flamboyant language and symbolism (Ezekiel 1-10). An angel foretells the future and interprets Zechariah's visions as the prophet encourages the exiles to rebuild the Temple in Jerusalem (Zechariah 1-8).

As Israel cries out more urgently for the Messiah, the Bible assumes more apocalyptic overtones and angels assume individual forms and names. For example, an angel subdues the flames for the three young men cast into the fiery furnace and the three call on the angels to "Bless the Lord" (Daniel 3:13-30). Daniel, thrust into the lion's den, is saved by an angel who tames the lion (Daniel 6:10-23). A "Meals-on-Angel's Wings" incident occurs as Habakkuk, transported by the hair of his head by an angel, delivers lunch for Daniel in the lion's den (Daniel 14:36).

The Maccabees, pious Jews at war with Syrians and Persians, describe in vivid imagery how mysterious horsemen in the sky waged war with the enemy. Though it is not mentioned explicitly that these were angels, the Jews believed their victories were due to heavenly interventions (2 Maccabees 3:24-30, 5:2-4, 10:29-30, 11:8).

Some angels in the Old Testament are actually mentioned by name: Michael, Gabriel, and Raphael for example. In Daniel, we see Michael as the chief prince of the heavenly host and guardian and protector of nations (Daniel 10:13, 12:1), who is believed to have led the attack on driving Satan out of heaven. The angel Gabriel appears twice to Daniel and interprets visions of the ram and goat and the seventy years of captivity (Daniel 8:16, 9:21). Angel Raphael intervenes most intimately in human affairs in the book of Tobit (Tobit 5:4-12:21). He appears as a young man named Azariah and aids God-fearing Tobit and his family. Angel Raphael, concerned for their welfare, acts as a journey companion, marriage arranger, exorcist, bill collector, healer, and host of a family reunion. When Raphael reveals his identity as "one of the seven angels who stand ready and enter before the glory of the Lord" (Tobit 12:15), he asks only that Tobit and his family give praise and thanks to God (Tobit 12:6-7).

In addition to specific names, angels are also ranked according to "class." The two highest classes of angels, seraphs (or seraphim) and cherubs (or cherubim) are cited in several Old Testament texts. Along with flaming swords, we find cherubim guarding the gate of Eden after Adam and Eve are ousted (Genesis 3:24). As golden images with outstretched wings, cherubim are commissioned by God to be placed by the Ark of the Covenant and in the Holy of Holies of Solomon's Temple (Exodus 25:10-22). Cherubs are the bearers of God and of divine glory in Ezekiel's visions (Ezekiel 9:3, 10:4).

Seraphs rank next to the heavenly throne and render constant praise to God. Isaiah is given a glimpse of their glory as they sing "Holy, holy, holy" (Isaiah 6:2-3) and one purifies the prophet with a burning coal (Isaiah 6:6-7).

The angels were known through their deeds and were associated with noble traits and desirable characteristics associated with the realm of the angels. As we reflect on the history of the people of Israel, we marvel how the Lord utilized the angels in so many ways in service and as mediators with the human race. As "messengers of Yahweh" who came in the guise of young men, a voice, or a presence, angels were intimately involved in human affairs and concerns in the Bible.

The angels came to the aid of human desperation swifter than a 911 call and, with mission accomplished, they disappeared. No human task was beneath the dignity of the heavenly envoys. Angels greeted, visited, accompanied, lead, protected, fed, fought, sang, and above all, praised God. They performed marvelous feats to prove that the work of the Lord surpassed in greatness humankind's expectations. Angels assumed the roles of magician, caterer, lion tamer, firefighter, journey companion, healer, water-power authority, travel agent, and traffic director. Throughout the pages of the Old Testament, the angels appeared as messengers and mediators of God; their mission focused in bringing God's message from heaven.

The Coming of Christ

With the coming of Christ, the angels' mission assumed a greater dimension—their praise now encompassed both heaven and earth.

The earth was graced with the heavenly host who adored the Son of God in human form. The angels put aside their mediation role in the Old Covenant to make room for the divine mediator, Jesus.

With the coming of Jesus, the earth itself was divinized, raised to a higher level, because God himself became an inhabitant. As a result, the angels became more closely bonded with the human race, ushering in not only a radical transformation for the angels' mission but a whole new theological orientation for us humans and our relationship with the angels.

Jesus not only dwelt among us but his redemptive death and resurrection graced us with the ability to share in the divine life that the angels already enjoyed. Because of Christ, angels and humans can enjoy a deeper spiritual relationship.

Angels in the New Testament

Angels of the New Testament appeared as messengers "sent by God." They inspired awe and usually prefaced the angelic salutation with "Fear not!" They were majestic, powerful, and glorious.

Angels play a prominent role in the opening chapters of Matthew's and Luke's Gospels. What would the Christmas story be without the angels surrounding the events of Christ's birth? Delete the angels from the infancy narratives, and the Christmas event would lose most of its charm and mystique.

From the beginning, the angels play a significant role. "The angel Gabriel was sent by God...to a virgin..." (Luke 1:26,27). Later, an "angel of the Lord" appears to

Joseph, informs him of Mary's pregnancy, and later warns him to flee to Egypt (Matthew 1:20, 2:13,20). The angel Gabriel also announces the birth of John the Baptist to Elizabeth and Zechariah (Luke 1:11-13).

The splendor of the heavenly host reaches full crescendo as they announce the birth of Christ to the shepherds, a favored image among all Christians: "There was with the angel a multitude of the heavenly host, praising God and saying, 'Glory to God in the highest heaven, / and on earth peace among those whom he favors!'" (Luke 2:13–14).

During Jesus' adult years, we see angels active in his public ministry. For example, angels comfort Jesus after his forty-day fast and ultimate temptation in the desert (Mark 1:13, Matthew 4:11). Jesus himself refers to angels in his ministry; he speaks about angels' protection of small children (Matthew 18:10), and provides insight into the spiritual nature of angels (Mark 12:25). Angels have their limitations, however, and do not know the future (Matthew 24:36). Jesus affirms that angels assist us at death just as they carried Lazarus to Abraham's bosom (Luke 16:22). Anyone who acknowledges Jesus will be acknowledged before God and the angels in heaven (Luke 12:8).

Legions of angels are at the service of Jesus (Matthew 26:53) and comfort him during his agony in the garden (Luke 22:43). Angels announce the Resurrection and witness to the risen Lord (Matthew 28:2-7, Luke 24:23, John 20:12-13).

Jesus prophesies that angels will accompany him at his second coming (Mark 8:38, Matthew 16:27, Luke 9:26) and will administer God's justice as they gather the elect on Judgment Day (Matthew 13:41, 24:31, Mark 13:27).

New Testament writings tell us that as the early Church developed, the marvelous works of Christ were continued by the Apostles. Angels guided the young Church and intervened in marvelous ways. We read that Peter and John, imprisoned because of their preaching and healings, are miraculously led out of prison by an angel who exhorts them to continue proclaiming the Good News (Acts of the Apostles 5:19-20). An angel frees Peter imprisoned by Herod (Acts 12:7-11).

With time, the young Christian community grew through the intervention of angels. An angel counsels Philip to pursue the Ethiopian eunuch who is instructed and baptized by Philip (Acts 8:26). The Christian community accepts outsiders through an angel who advises Cornelius to seek out Peter who brings him and his household into the faith (Acts 10:3-48). Angels protect the young community from danger by striking the adversary, Herod Agrippa, with a deadly disease (Acts 12:23). While sailing to Rome, Paul meets up with a severe storm, but an angel assures him that he will reach port safely, even though the ship will be lost (Acts 27:23-24).

In the epistles, Paul speaks of angels from a theological view. He compares Jesus' supremacy to the angels' mission: "To which of the angels did God ever say, 'You are my Son...'" (Hebrews 1:4-14). Paul also influenced later angelology which lists the choirs of angels. In Ephesians 1:21 and Colossians 1:16 Paul makes reference to most of the choirs of angels; other choirs are named in other books of the Bible.

New Testament authors often emphasized the role angels will play in the Second Coming of Christ. In preparation for the Second Coming with the angels at the end of time, Paul exhorts Christians to fidelity (2 Thessalonians 1:7-8). In the Epistle to the Hebrews and throughout the Book of Revelation, angels are seen in their full splendor, as the heavenly host take part in the Second Coming and the Judgment. The angelic panorama reaches its climax and full majesty as they join with those who are saved in the "city of the living God, the heavenly Jerusalem" (Hebrews 12:22).

Clearly, Scripture provides sufficient evidence to confirm our belief in the existence of angels. We are also privileged with an understanding of their mission. By their works we get a glimpse of the role angels played, then and now: agents and messengers of God's divine plan.

In addition to the Scripture references that form the basis for our belief in angels, the Church further clarifies what God has revealed about angels through solemn dogmas of faith. Although dogmatic statements concerning angels are few, the Church sets down in broad outline the unchangeable truths that we assent to as Catholics.

As we begin this reflection, it is imperative that we know specifically what the Catholic Church has dogmatically proclaimed concerning the angels. What we know over and above the dogmatic truths and traditional teachings belongs to the realm of theological speculation.

Dogmas of the Catholic Church Concerning Angels

The Council of Nicaea in A.D. 325 formulated the truths of faith in the Nicene Creed. Although angels are not specifically mentioned, their existence and creation are implied in the opening sentence: "We believe in God…Creator…of all that is seen and unseen…." Other dogmas regarding angels were defined in later Councils. For example, the Church explicitly defined dogmas concerning angels at the Fourth Lateran Council (1215) and again at the First Vatican Council (1870). These Councils declared that angels are spiritual beings with intelligence and free will created by God at the dawn of creation. The good angels, those who remained faithful, enjoy the Beatific Vision, glorify God, and are utilized by God as emissaries of the divine plan to humans.

The Church has also defined as dogma that some angels, led by Satan, rebelled and are forever cast out of God's presence. These fallen angels or devils have not lost their power to tempt human beings. Though there will be a constant struggle between good and evil, good will ultimately prevail because of Christ's redemption.

The Nicene Creed and the Teachings of Councils

Although our belief in angels is secondary to our belief in Christ, the Church teaches that the Lord uses angels to communicate his will to us mortal creatures. The Church affirms that Christ is the center of our worship, and that angels are "created through him and for him" (Colossians 1:16). The Lateran Synod (745) decreed that only those three angels mentioned by name in Scripture (Michael, Gabriel, and Raphael) are to be honored in the Church and its liturgy.

Traditional Beliefs Not Officially Declared Dogmas

The belief that each person and nation has an individual guardian angel is a longstanding tradition, but it has never been defined as a dogma. Likewise, the exact nature of the sin of the fallen angels, although it has been speculated upon, has never been dogmatically defined. Although we could elaborate more on the fallen angels, this work concentrates on the role of the good angels in our life.

Catechism of the Catholic Church

The *Catechism of the Catholic Church* explains the Church's teaching on angels in paragraphs 326-336, 350-352, and 391-393. The resources cited include Sacred Scripture, Saint Augustine, Saint Thomas Aquinas, and the Fourth Lateran Council.

As we reflect on the mission and role angels play in human affairs, our sense of wonder can be as real as was my experience of my angel as a child. Our challenge today is to affirm the belief that the will of God continues to be revealed with the heavenly assistance of angels. What we accept in faith and dogma, we allow to develop into a sincere love for the angelic presence in our lives.

Conclusion

Let us be open to God's grace in our lives and respond to it in faith. Much of what we believe about angels cannot be humanly understood. When it comes to exploring the angelic realms, we must be content to live with the element of mystery. Yet we thank the Lord when we get a closer glimpse.

PART II

Angels in Tradition and Theology

Our prayers are so dear to God, that he has appointed the angels to present them to him as soon as they come forth from our mouths.

Saint Alphonsus Liguori

M ark Twain once quipped that he was born "excited." That statement can be applied to all of us. We are born with an ardent desire to learn about and discover the world around us. We need only look around to see how our innate yen to explore has caused drastic changes in lifestyle and opened new vistas.

Human curiosity and interest in the visible world lead us to wonder about the invisible world of the spirit. Although we learn basic truths about God and our religion, we remain unsatisfied. We continue to question.

Theology attempts to answer our questions by opening up wider horizons and deeper insights about the spiritual world. Theology is "faith in search of understanding." Since spiritual matters deal with another dimension of being, our human language is limited. We can explain supernatural mysteries only by references to familiar realities. Through theological speculation and scholarly research, the Church more clearly articulates the revealed truths of faith.

Angelology

Angelology is our attempt to understand more about angels. Although it is not as extensive as other branches of theology, angelology sheds light on the angelic realm.

Attempting to explain ideas about angels in human language is like trying to get shortwave radio signals with an AM receptor. Because angels and humans are on different "wavelengths" and in different dimensions of reality, angelology relies on analogies to help us understand. As we page through our Church history of two thousand years, we see how angels have inspired peoples of every age. Yet we do not know everything we would like to know.

Much of what theologians teach about angels is based on Scripture and theological inquiry. Some speculations are based in tradition, so much so that they are part of our faith heritage. Tracing the development of the Catholic

teachings on angels, summarizing the teaching of Saint Thomas Aquinas, and exploring some unresolved speculations will help clarify what we do know about angels.

The Early Church Fathers (A.D. 100–500)

In the early Church, angels were an accepted truth of faith because their existence was revealed by God in Scripture. When the Council of Nicaea formulated the Nicene Creed, belief in angels was included in the first article: "Creator…of all that is seen and unseen." Angels were taken for granted as part of the deposit of faith, but their nature was not debated or explored any further. For several hundred years after Christ, theologians focused their theological inquiries mainly on the Trinity and on the nature of Jesus.

The early writers and Fathers of the Church, however, had a deep awareness of angels and acknowledged their protective presence. Specific treatises about angels were few, but devotion to angels, especially guardian angels, was encouraged and included in letters and exhortations. Saints Ambrose, Jerome, and Gregory compiled lists of the choirs of angels. Liturgical texts from this period mention angels as actively present at liturgy, especially at baptisms.

Saint Augustine, Bishop of Hippo (A.D. 354–430)

Augustine was the first theologian to collate the truths of faith. Although he included references to angels in his two great works (*Confessions* and *City of God*), he gave most of his study to the human condition; he did not delve into the metaphysics of angels' existence. For Augustine, angels are to be accepted in faith, not to be questioned by human reasoning.

In *City of God* Augustine viewed the fulfillment of the kingdom of God as a time when earthly pilgrims will attain eternal glory and join with the angels and saints in praise of God forever. He claimed that we know about angels through their function as messengers, and not through their nature, which is spirit. He also believed that every visible thing in the world is in the charge of an angel. Later theologians, of course, disagreed with some of Augustine's conclusions.

An anonymous sixth century Syrian monk, who called himself Dionysius after a disciple of Paul, explained the heavens and earth with the Neo-Platonist notion of an ordered hierarchy. Pseudo-Dionysius, as he is known, viewed all of creation as being bonded in successive stages from the lowliest creature on earth to the highest in heaven. In *The Celestial Hierarchy*, he arranged the angels into nine choirs in a gradual ascent to God's heavenly throne. His listing of angel choirs, adopted by Thomas Aquinas, is still recognized in Christian angelology.

Pseudo-Dionysius (circa A.D. 500)

The tenth through the fourteenth centuries brought monumental intellectual progress as universities sprang up and specialized in medicine, law, and theology. Ordinary lay people who did not attend formal university classes, however, learned and received information by listening to lectures given by expert professors. Remember, this was before the printing press made books more available. Scholars and philosophers gathered an audience, expatiated on a topic, answered questions, and responded to objections. This method was the "spectator sport" of the Middle Ages.

One of the scholars who participated in this manner of sharing knowledge was Thomas Aquinas, a professor at the University of Paris.

The Middle Ages

Thomas Aquinas, a Dominican friar, is known for his work in synthesizing all Christian truths in his work titled *Summa Theologica*. The genius of Thomas lies in his ability to combine God's revelation with human reasoning and logic, drawn from the Greek philosophers, especially Aristotle.

Thomas Aquinas (A.D. 1225– 1274)

Thomas did not base his findings on mystical experiences, as had some saints. Rather Thomas explained mysteries of faith by using logical reasoning. He explained deep theological concepts in clear, succinct terms, comparing supernatural beliefs to elements of human experience.

In setting forth an ordered system of Christian doctrine, Thomas used Greek philosophy, not as a ladder to ascend to God, but more like a scaffold that revealed the presence of God behind all realities. Although he emphasized the intellectual aspect of faith, Thomas saw God as the First Cause and Source of all creation. He saw no discrepancy between faith and reason, for both are rooted in God.

In 1259 Thomas gave a series of lectures on angels which was later incorporated into his *Summa Theologica*. Thomas responded to questions about angels by blending philosophic principles with revealed truths. In so doing, he delved deep into the angelic realm—deeper than anyone had ever ventured. As a result, Thomas has been called the "angelic doctor," and rightly so, because his theories about angels have been accepted as the standard Catholic angelology.

The existence of angels: Thomas realized that the very existence of angels is revealed by God in Scripture. Human reason cannot prove the existence of angels, but reason can explain the possibility of their existence. According to Thomistic thought, God's creation exists in successive stages of perfection, specifically three levels of existence: material, spiritual, and a combination of material and spiritual, as manifested in the human species.

Angels exist, Thomas concluded, because the universe would be incomplete without pure spiritual beings. Angels exist as buffers between God and humans. Made in the image and likeness of God, angels are the most excellent of God's creatures because they most closely resemble the nature of God.

Thomas also concluded that all the angels were created simultaneously, thus it can be surmised that no angel is older than another. Angels are not eternal, however; God alone is eternal. Rather, angels are immortal, like the human soul. Although we cannot calculate the number of angels, Scripture tells us that their number is "legion." They do not multiply, nor will they cease to exist. They were created like the rest of the world, out of nothing and before Adam and Eve.

The role, mission, and nature of angels: Predating Copernicus and Galileo, Thomas accepted the geocentric concept of the universe: the earth is the center. His teachings on angels reflect this belief. According to Thomas, the mission and role of angels is to worship and adore God, to communicate God's plan to humans, and to act as guardians and protectors. That angels protect us and have a sincere interest in our human welfare are beliefs that go back to biblical times. Thomas reasoned that God designated angels to be in charge of every material part of creation.

Although Thomas explained the nature of angels by using the same concepts he used to explained human nature, he acknowledged that the nature of the angels is radically different from human existence. As pure spirits, angels are more like God than humans. They never become human, however, nor do humans become angels after death.

Since angels are pure spirits, not partitioned by matter, each angel is its own distinct species and has no body, although it may assume human form when appearing to humans. Thomas and others who explored this phenomenon, however, never agreed on the nature of this assumed body.

Angels are not impersonal forces or centers of energy.

They are personal, powerful realities, the highest level of creatures, next to God in perfection. Because angels have no bodies, they do not rely on a physical mind or on physical senses. They are endowed with great intelligence, yet their knowledge is purely intuitive and exceeds human understanding. Angels are not omniscient or cognizant of the future. They know only what God allows them to know. Remember what Jesus said about the angels not knowing the time of Christ's Second Coming.

The angels' freedom and will: Thomas reasons that angels, as pure intellect, have a will that is totally free, but not without limits. Angels can make no judgment; they cannot reason through a problem. Angels who have freely chosen good, by their definitive choice, are confirmed forever in virtue. Love is perfected in the good angels, and so moral decisions are unnecessary.

Angels' communication and relationships: Because our senses are our means of experiencing the world around us, it's hard to imagine the nature of angelic activity. Thomas concluded that angels communicate with each other merely by directing their thoughts. Although angels can be in only one place at a time, they can move at will as rapidly as does human thought.

Not only do angels guard us, but angels influence and enlighten us, although we are not aware of the angelic inspiration. The good angels respect our freedom; the fallen angels do not and so try to cajole us into sin.

Fallen angels: All angels were created good by God at the moment of creation. To merit eternal happiness the angels needed to exercise their freedom by actively desiring union with God. Since angels are endowed with intuitive knowledge and determinant will, they were given only one unretractable chance to choose good or evil. Those who chose evil did so freely and decisively. We do not know the exact nature of the test, although many theories have been proposed. Some scholars, including Thomas Aquinas, suggest that all the angels were given knowledge of the Son of God becoming man.

By refusing to take part in building up the kingdom of God, the rebellious angels are bound eternally by their choice. Although they continue to suffer the penalties of their sin, their capacity to tempt humans has not been denied them. The fallen angels, or devils, influence our human imagination and present evil as an attractive choice. Although the devil retains a limited dominion over the world, he lures humans into sin. Out of jealousy for our human capacity for goodness and holiness, he often attacks to the point of completely dominating us by diabolic possession. Although the Church is cautious about this phenomenon, it believes possession by the devil is possible and has sanctioned the rite of exorcism to be used in extreme cases by authorized exorcists.

Even Jesus did not escape the devil's temptation. In his first epistle, Peter admonishes: "Discipline yourselves, keep alert. Like a roaring lion your adversary the devil prowls around, looking for someone to devour" (1 Peter 5:8).

Thomas conjectures that the number of fallen angels is fewer than the good angels, who are settled in holiness for eternity.

The angelic hierarchy: Thomas viewed the world as a hierarchy and accepted Pseudo-Dionysius' division of angels into nine choirs. The nine choirs of angels, all mentioned in Scripture, correspond to the degree of perfection and the task entrusted to the angels in God's designs. Theologians speculated further and subdivided the choirs into three groups, determined by the angels' roles and functions.

The following list is standard in Christian angelology:

First Group
Seraphim, Cherubim, Thrones

Second Group
Dominations, Virtues, Powers

Third Group
Principalities, Archangels, Angels

Seraphim, Cherubim, and Thrones, the highest order of angels, are closest to God and worship God around the heavenly throne.

The second triad governs the universe. These angels are said to preserve order and carry out God's will in the cosmos.

Principalities, Archangels, and Angels, the lowest order, deal directly with earth by communicating God's plan and by protecting and guarding human beings.

Conclusion to Thomistic Angelology

The above theories set forth by Thomas Aquinas have become the norm for Catholic teachings about angels. Although Aquinas' theories have survived hundreds of years, his philosophic emphasis had not always been accepted without debate because he was accused of relying too heavily upon human reasoning. He was a staunch proponent of Scholasticism, a method of intellectual inquiry popular in medieval Western thought. This system sought to clarify the revealed truths of faith through logic, reasoning, and precise language modeled on Greek philosophy.

Sometimes, however, the human imagination ran wild when explaining abstruse theological concepts, such as "How many angels can dance on the head of a pin?" Angelologists contend that this query was not a serious concern in the Middle Ages, but was a theological fine point brought up in ridicule of former speculations.

Various schools of thought also were in competition

as well as in contradiction with each other. Thomas Aquinas, a Dominican, was not without rivals—most notably the Franciscans, Duns Scotus and Bonaventure.

Despite its limits, however, Thomistic thought has prevailed after being ignored for several hundred years. The Council of Trent (1545–1563) did not pronounce new doctrines on angels, but confirmed existing dogmas and beliefs. The assembly also affirmed Thomas Aquinas as one of the authoritative resources of Catholic theology; he is still respected today for his contributions to Christian thought.

The Renaissance brought a rebirth of ideas as well as a drastic change in the way people viewed the world. It was an age of discoveries and inventions, when humans were learning to control and harness the forces of nature. Society was gripped with fascination for the natural world and human intellectual potential.

The Renaissance (1300–1500)

This shift of emphasis greatly affected religious thought. Religious faith was expressed through human imagination and experience. Belief in and devotion to angels was expressed through human creativity.

Philosophic speculation about the angelic world gave way to imaginative portrayals of angels in the arts, making angels "visible." Mystics recounted their angelic experiences through detailed descriptions while artists, musicians, writers, and sculptors portrayed angels with human characteristics in graphic imagery. The cultural contributions of the Renaissance, which affect us even today, are discussed in greater length in Part III.

As the world entered the phase of discovery and inventions, human interests shifted to worldly progress. The discoveries of Copernicus and Galileo concerning the sun as the center of the solar system upset the medieval world-view and greatly affected theological theories. As for the Church, it did not explain its doc-

Late Middle Ages/Early Modern Era

trines philosophically, but took a defensive stance against the opposition of the Reformation.

The Age of Enlightenment focused on the natural world and human reasoning. Scientific and industrial progress practically ignored religion and, in some cases, was hostile toward anything spiritual. Supernatural experiences and phenomena were held suspect.

People did not totally lose their religiosity, however. They practiced their religion through popular devotions, which brought about another phase in the development of angelology: angels became objects of piety and devotion. Prayers, novenas, guilds, and devotions to angels sprang up. Toward the close of the nineteenth century, after a religious experience concerning the power of evil in the world, Pope Leo XIII ordered a prayer to Saint Michael be recited after each low mass. This practice was in effect until the liturgical changes of the Second Vatican Council.

Twentieth Century Popes and the Second Vatican Council

Most of the popes of the twentieth century did not hesitate to credit angels for their guidance. In defense of an error that circulated about angels as impersonal forces, Pius XII taught that angels are created personal beings (*Of the Human Race*, [*Humani Generis*], 1950).

Pope John XXIII attributed inspiration for the Second Vatican Council (1962–1965) to the Holy Spirit and to his angel. Attempting to keep the Church abreast of the modern age, Vatican II was more pastoral than dogmatic. It focused mainly on the Church's presence in the world as a relevant witness to God's plan in our modern era.

Although the Council made no specific declarations concerning angels, it briefly referred to angels as it affirmed the communion of saints and the martyrs' share in eternal joy "with the Blessed Virgin Mary and the holy angels" (*Dogmatic Constitution on the Church*, #50).

In 1986, Pope John Paul II, a Thomistic scholar, delivered a series of lectures on the catechesis of angels.

He referred to angels as a necessary part of our belief. If we get rid of angels, the pontiff observed, we radically alter the whole history of salvation.

As we launch further into space and see how vast the universe is, cosmic discoveries make us wonder whether there is intelligent life on other celestial bodies. While science fiction graphically portrays the world of the future, our imaginations ponder the very real possibility of interstellar life. Consider, for example, the furor raised by a purported UFO sighting.

Current Interest in Angels

This speculation leaves us with some modern "wonderings" about the angels. Are there other material beings living on other celestial bodies, beings whose intelligence ranges between ours and the angels we embrace in our faith life? Are other celestial bodies home to other creatures, possibly more intelligent than the human species? Might these creatures be the angels?

Do angels make themselves visible and come to aid us in the guise of strangers? Because of the seemingly increased number of angel-encounter reports, are angels more active in our world today—or are we simply more attentive to the world of the spirit?

Whatever is true, we hold to the belief that there is a purely spiritual world of angels, who praise God and have a vested interest in us earthly beings.

Conclusion

We may have harnessed the energy of the sun, scaled the heights of space, and delved deep into earth's wonders, but we still are creatures, human and limited. We may feel closer to angels the more we know about them, but angels continue to be mysteries of faith.

Our dignity, "a little lower than God, / and crowned …with glory and honor" (Psalm 8:5), enables us to share in God's life with the angels. Till then, we continue to believe in the existence of angels as revealed by God yet not completely understood by us in our present state.

For unbelievers and skeptics, no wondrous work or miracle will ever be convincing proof of angels. For those who believe in angels, no concrete evidence is demanded. God's word is enough: "'What no eye has seen, nor ear heard, / nor the human heart conceived, / what God has prepared for those who love him'— / these things God has revealed to us through the Spirit" (1 Corinthians 2:9-10).

Angels are more than theological conclusions or doctrines of faith. They are personal beings with whom we can establish a close and loving relationship and who assist us in our spiritual journey toward our eternal goal.

PART III

Angels in Human Imagination and Creativity

Make yourself familiar with the angels
and behold them frequently in spirit;
for without being seen, they are present with you.

Saint Francis de Sales

W hat would life be like without our senses? We would miss out on many things life has to offer. As an indispensable part of our makeup, our senses enable us to see, hear, taste, feel, and smell that which is present to us. Our senses allow us to experience life in its many splendid dimensions.

Often, however, we go through life passively, taking our senses for granted. We are like those castigated by the psalmist: "They have…eyes, but do not see. / They have ears, but do not hear; / noses, but do not smell. / They have hands, but do not feel" (Psalm 115:5-7). If we do not allow sensory stimuli to enter our consciousness, our senses grow stale. Only by stopping to smell the roses along the path of life do we enrich our life experience.

Over and above the senses, we are gifted with our imagination, which interprets that which is present and brings into focus that which is not seen. With our imagination, we can experience the unseen, those splendid realities of another time and dimension. We are more fully human when we use our imagination, for we thereby participate in the ongoing process of creation.

Remember how as a child your imagination ran wild with all sorts of creative notions. As adults, we need preserve this same imaginative bent if we are to enhance our understanding of the world around us. In nurturing our imaginative spirit and innate sense of wonder, we capture unseen realities in art, literature, and music.

God realized that mortals cannot relate meaningfully to abstractions, so "the Word was made flesh and dwelt among us." In the same fashion, angels are enfleshed among us and made more real and visible to us through the arts as readily as they flit through the pages of Scripture.

We owe a debt of gratitude to those artists, poets, and musicians who have made angels a more tangible reality for us through creative endeavors.

Our Senses and Our Imagination

Angels, Senses, and Human Imagination

My Personal Sensory Experience of Angels

To fully capture angels through the senses, and to practice what I preach, I first "experienced" this chapter. I opened my senses to the angelic world through my creative imagination.

First, I surrounded myself with angelic images; my office became a veritable angel museum. All surfaces served as display areas for a multitude of angel figurines. File drawers bulged with angel pictures; the sweet scent of incense streaming from the chapel nearby added to the celestial experience. I delved into master authors, inviting them to inspire me with their literature, poems, and stories that include angels. I played classical music which added a bit of heaven to my workplace. Angelic elegance was not hard to imagine as I watched ballet and ice dancers gracefully perform routines. I, too, feebly attempted to simulate angelic grace as I glided across the floor in aerobic rhythm. To top off my angelic sensory experiences I enjoyed an appropriate sweet: angel food cake.

Angels are more real to me since I have seen, heard, touched, smelled, and tasted that which we in our imagination associate with angels. These sensory exercises I experienced proved to me that angels are truly "messengers of joy."

Angels in Art

We fashion our image of angels according to ideals we envision in them, such as purity and innocence, strength and holiness. Adding to those envisioned ideals, artistic expressions of angels are influenced by culture and the personal vision of the artist.

As I surrounded myself with angel images and critically observed classical art, I tried to see as the artist saw—and the exercise proved eye-opening. I now look at angels with a renewed sight, with the eyes of discernment. I am amazed at the many variations we humans have imposed on angelic beings. We have put them everywhere: in frescoes, murals, stained glass, sculptures, paintings, tapestries, embroideries.

How do you imagine an angel? Think of that image, or better yet, sketch it. No matter what your image is like, your angel probably has certain traits common to most images of angels. Your angel is probably graceful, human in form, and probably has wings and a halo. One artist portrayed an angel as only a halo and wings.

Human form: Because we believe that angels have the same creative Source and common destiny as we do, we naturally image them as humans in our own likeness. With that natural bent, along with Thomas Aquinas' teaching that angels can assume any form, our imaginations have captured a great deal of creative angelic expressions.

But it wasn't always so. Before the Second Council of Nicaea in 787, many people considered the creation of sacred images to be heresy. The budding of angel art around the ninth century reached its full flowering in the Renaissance, from the fourteenth to the seventeenth centuries.

Since angels took on human forms in Scripture, most biblical paintings represented angels as strong, virile, stern, male youths. When angel art became more common in churches, angels took on a more androgynous appearance: neither male nor female.

Great masters, such as Raphael, Michelangelo, da Vinci and Fra Angelico, blended theological truths with their artistic genius and produced some of the world's greatest works. Softer, gentler features brought forth a sense of caring and healing, and gradually added a femininity to angels in art.

Modeled on Roman mythology's Cupid, infant angels developed as an innovation in Renaissance art. They were called *putti* (Italian) or "cherubs," a derivative of "cherubim," because they symbolized innocence and purity. These diminutive heavenly beings became popular about the time Christmas creches appeared. It seemed

most natural to surround the Christ Child with angels his own size.

In the sixteenth century, as artists attempted to emphasize angelic wisdom, angels in art began appearing with only infant heads and wings. The Victorian era secularized angels, portraying them as dimpled, chubby-cheeked, and blond. In surrealistic art, angels have been represented as translucent and wispy, indefinable and abstract.

Halos: Since angels are associated with divinity and holiness, they are often pictured with an ethereal halo of light, their whole being engulfed in brilliance. In representing the angels as human with godlike qualities, artists usually position halos encircled around their angels' heads. Sometimes the artist prefers a tiara or headband instead of a halo.

Wings: Wings, the most distinguishing mark of an angel, are symbolic accoutrements. Not circumscribed in time and space, nor bogged down by a material body, angels sporting wings aptly signify the angels' spiritual nature and transcendence. Aquinas taught that angels exist in that place where their thoughts are, so wings give the apt illusion of alacrity and speed.

Wings were not ordinarily connected with the "messenger of the Lord" in Scripture, where they were usually imaged as young men. Winged angels do, however, appear in the Bible. Winged cherubim are sentinels over the ark of the Covenant (Exodus 25:22) and spread their wings in the Holy of Holies (1 Kings 6:24). Ezekiel graphically describes winged cherubim in his tenth chapter.

Angels appeared with wings in Christian art in the fourth century, after Constantine began building churches. Artists employed wings to distinguish between their representations of the saints and their images of the angels. Winged angels were modeled after Nike, the Greek goddess of victory. Wings attached to angels' backs usually looked like the wings of large elegant birds: eagles, swans, and geese. Some archangels were depicted with decorative peacock-feather wings. Cherubs were usually given wings of small birds or diminutive butterfly-shaped wings. Note the moth-like wings of Raphael's two cherubs in the "Sistine Madonna," for example.

Wings were usually positioned on an angel to indicate flight. Angels kneeling in adoration with wings crossed over their faces symbolized the hidden mystery of the Divine. When angels were communicating a divine message they were shown with wings at rest at their sides.

A scientist observed that wings given to angels are contrary to the laws of aerodynamics. Nonetheless, wings will remain an angelic hallmark.

Angelic attire and colors: Although angel fashions have remained rather constant over the years, we can determine the era of a piece of art by what the angel is wearing. Sometimes, of course, angel garb is obscured because the angelic figure may be engulfed in brightness and light.

It is common to see angels in loose, flowing alb-like garments gathered at the waist with a sash. In classical art, angels were often attired in elegant robes indicative of a specific culture. While Renaissance art often depicted angels dressed in priestly robes and vestments, Victorian angels were clothed in contemporary garb with laces and ribbons. Chubby cherubs were usually scantily clad, or even naked.

Just as color plays a major symbolic role in Christian liturgy, color has been symbolic in angel art. Colors signify a deeper value. The color most commonly associated with angels is white, brilliant and glowing, to match their wispy, flowing robes.

Early Christian art represented angels as regal and

majestic, so angels were clothed in deep purple or royal blue, especially in Eastern rite icons. The seraphim were generally pictured in blue, denoting wisdom, and the cherubim were clad in red, indicating majesty. Angels' robes often were outlined in gold, especially in Renaissance art. Feminine and dainty angels, such as the Victorian variety, were garbed in wispy pastels. There are no fast rules, however, for style or color; artistic license has always allowed such detail to be the artist's choice.

Bodily stance, facial expressions, and gestures: Psychology tells us that we often can "read a person like a book" through body language. In angel art, we can recognize what the artist wished to portray by observing the angels' stance, expressions, and gestures.

Since angels belong to the celestial realm, they often were pictured floating or soaring upward, as in scenes proclaiming Christ's birth to the shepherds. To depict in one glance both angelic innocence and godliness, artists often posed chubby cherubs sitting on fluffy, marshmallow-like clouds.

As angels gained popularity, artists placed them at ground level, in direct eye contact with human beings, as noted in various works that focus on the Annunciation. Most often angels were expressed in motion: standing, kneeling, flying, or walking. We rarely see the image of an angel sitting or lying down.

Since the face mirrors one's being, artists often gave their angels various facial expressions to convey a certain disposition or attitude. Early art portrayed the angels solemn and stern, perhaps because of the serious message angels bore from the Lord. "Fear not" was a common introductory greeting of angels in the Bible.

Downcast eyes and bowed heads portrayed a stance of adoration. As theology during the Middle Ages sought to make the heavenly messengers more approachable and attractive, angels' facial expressions were more direct.

Softer, gentler angels wore kind, friendly expressions wreathed in loving smiles.

As angels assumed infant features, they became darling, dimpled Shirley Temple images, illustrating innocence, sweetness, and grace. Their large expressive eyes were filled with childlike wonder and awe.

We also sense a great deal about an angel, and the artist's intentions, by noting how the angel's hands are positioned: clasped in prayer, extended in praise, crossed over the breast in adoration, or holding some symbolic object. Outstretched arms in the stance of announcing were common in art, such as those masterpieces that capture the moment of the Annunciation. Especially memorable is a work of art that depicts the Agony in Gethsemane, in which an angel cradles Jesus' head in a comforting embrace.

Symbols: Angels never came empty-handed before the Lord. If their hands were not clasped in prayer or extended in praise, they were holding something. These accessories symbolized the angels' mission and role, and denoted an attribute the artist wished to portray.

Since we perceive angels to be musically inclined by nature, many artists placed musical instruments or song books in their angels' hands as they play and sing before the Lord. Based on descriptions from the Bible, angels were often pictured with harps, lutes, or trumpets. Renaissance art added other instruments to the angels' orchestra: viols, flutes, mandolins, tambourines, cymbals. No musical instrument seemed beneath angelic ability, although I haven't come across any image of an angel playing a tuba.

Angels held scepters and orbs to symbolize power. Olive branches borne by angels offered a visual statement of hope, especially a hope for peace. To depict angelic wisdom and intelligence, artists placed scrolls in their angels' hands. Sometimes angels were pictured with a censor, as they offer incense to the Lord. Banners or streamers emblazoned with "peace and good will" were—and remain—common in nativity scenes. In popular art, angels carry candles and flowers and other objects deemed appropriate.

The three archangels honored by Catholics are represented in art with apt symbols that signify their specific biblical functions and roles. For example, Michael, the warrior angel, depicted as slaying the dragon or casting demons out of heaven, was clothed in armor and shield, brandishing a spear or sword. Gabriel, the angel of the Annunciation, was pictured with a lily or scroll. Since Gabriel is believed to be the angel who will herald the Second Coming of Christ, he has been depicted on weather vanes facing east. This was common in nineteenth-century America when millenialist movements thrived. Raphael, the guide of Tobias, has been pictured shod with sandals and carrying a wallet, water jug, or traveler's staff.

No matter what form angels assume or how art depicts them, angels in art leave us with a spiritual uplift and serenity. We feel we know them better after seeing them in images.

Angels in Classical Art   The following cross section of angel art is especially inspiring:

The "Sistine Madonna": Raphael's angel cherubs lean on the bottom margin of his "Sistine Madonna," looking so real with their tousled hair and winsome look. We are tempted to pinch their cheeks and give them a squeeze as we do to lovable youngsters. They are a popular image, so popular that they are featured on the Love-series postage stamp.

"The Immaculate Conception": Cherubs form an angelic-garland wreath around Mary in this famous work by Murillo.

"The Virgin with Angels": This masterpiece by the French artist W. Bouguereau depicts youthful angels garbed in flowing white with pure white wings gazing on Mary and Child in adoration.

"Creation": Who is not astounded at the majestic fresco by Michelangelo on the dome of the Sistine Chapel. After the larger-than-life figures were painted in the "Creation," Michelangelo filled in the contoured corners with diminutive angels.

"Angels": This work by the Flemish painter Gerard David portrays a group of angels in flight. The angels' grace, power, and speed are captured with oversized wings, an often-used technique of Renaissance artists.

"The Three Archangels and Tobias": This rare Renaissance masterpiece by Francesco Botticini features the three archangels. Young Tobias, grasping the hand of Raphael, is dwarfed by the archangels, who are clothed appropriate to their missions and carry the symbols connected with them.

"Nativity": Guido de Pietro, a pupil of Fra Angelico, chooses the setting at the mouth of the cave where Jesus was born. Eleven angels above the cave are smaller in size than the main figures, each with different garb, facial expression, and hand gesture. Dominant are the halos and auras of the angels and the Child, done with hammered gold leaf.

"Dante and Beatrice Among the Circles of Angels": The illustrations of Gustave Dore, the French artist for *Paradise Lost* and *The Divine Comedy*, help us visualize the verbal imagery of those literary masterpieces.

William Blake: This English artist, poet, and mystic, who is said to have experienced a "tree full of angels," contributed realistic yet radiantly ethereal art to angel-ology. Especially touching are his "Jacob's Dream," "Angels Keeping Watch Over Innocent Adam and Eve Asleep," and "Angels Watching Over Christ."

"Angel Musicians": Angels as musicians was a popular theme of Fra Angelico, Melozzo de Forli, and Hans Memlinc. Their angel musicians are interesting studies in contrasts, from Memlinc's stern masculine-featured angels to the gentle feminine beauty of Forli's angels. Personally, I prefer the elegance and grace of Fra Angelico's "Angel Musicians."

"Lamentation": This emotionally gripping work by Giotto depicts the dead body of Christ surrounded by loved ones. Eleven angels hovering above dramatically display their grief: writhing in anguish, sobbing, and even tearing out their hair.

Until I delved into angel art I didn't realize the many "Annunciation" works in existence, mostly produced during the Renaissance, when popular devotion to Mary and the angels was at a high point. I was especially fas-cinated when I compared Lorenzo Monaco's "Gabriel" rendered as an ethereal, floating angel (1420) to Fra Angelico's "Annunciation," that captures exquisite and realistic body detail (1435). In the latter, the angel's hands are positioned as if speaking, and the gilded words "Ave Maria…" pour forth from Gabriel's mouth. Mary's reply, "Ecce ancilla domini" (Behold the handmaid of the Lord), is inscribed upside down so that God can read it.

Conclusion   As I ponder my angel gallery, I know that I will never again look at a picture of an angel in quite the same way. I have conditioned myself to note the angelic trait the artists wish to depict. Each piece of art is a unique gift, allowing angels a share in our world.

What does an angel really look like? We still don't know. We do have a better sense, however, for what angels mean to us. The images and art works of angels elicit from us an act of faith and inspire us toward deeper reverence and devotion—and that is enough.

Angels in Literature

The written word, unlike art, forces us to exercise our imagination to "see" what is related. Great writers have painted vivid, verbal pictures that make unseen worlds come alive on the printed page. The creative genius of authors, poets, and storytellers have given us a glimpse into that mysterious world where angels skip, dance, sing, and pray. Granted, their footsteps fall only across the printed page, but the impact remains powerful, insightful, and timeless.

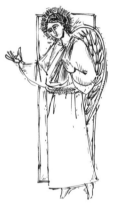

Two authors in whose works angels figure prominently are John Milton and Dante Alighieri.

John Milton (1608–1674): Angels are central to the theme of John Milton's *Paradise Lost*. This literary classic, a twelve-volume work said to be the greatest epic in English, was dictated by Milton late in life when he was blind.

The epic focuses on two momentous events in the human and angelic worlds: the expulsion of the demons into hell, and the life and expulsion of Adam and Eve from Paradise. Milton abundantly sprinkles angels throughout these cataclysmic moments, saying that millions of these spiritual creatures walk the earth unseen, while we're awake and while we sleep.

Milton contrasts the celestial joy of angels with the human plight of limitations and propensity to sin. Angels are saddened by the plight of human sin, but realize the hope of redemption. Although the bad angels are the protagonists, the archangels are friendly compan-

ions, mentors, and executors of justice for Adam and Eve—frail human beings compared to the power of Satan and the fallen angels. Eden symbolizes perfection, but the idyllic innocence is seen under the shadow of evil.

The epic concludes as Adam and Eve leave Paradise. Even though there is the promise of redemption, the two wander in the real world, where there is a constant conflict between good and evil.

Dante Alighieri (1265–1321): Do you really want to know what the angels do and how they live? Do you want to get a glimpse into the angelic lifestyle? No other writer provides celestial insights better than the Florentine poet, Dante.

The Divine Comedy is an allegory in which Dante journeys through the three states of existence in the afterlife: hell, purgatory, and heaven. Dante, a wandering pilgrim, is guided through the nine regions of hell and the seven circles of purgatory by Virgil, the classic poet who symbolizes human reason. Dante then enters the original Eden and is met by his idealized love, Lady Beatrice, the symbol of goodness and graciousness, who leads Dante to the celestial expanses of the heavens. Bernard of Clairvaux, the symbol of contemplation, introduces Dante to Mary, the Queen of Heaven, before the highest heaven, where dwells Absolute Divine Love, the Blessed Trinity.

Dante challenges his reader to a spiritual outlook on life that climaxes in the ultimate goal of human existence: beatitude with Divine Love. Dante gives us not only a glimpse of the afterlife but a panoramic view of all human history. He answers bigger-than-life questions through noted personalities who have left their footprints on the sands of medieval times. Well-versed in the philosophies and theologies of the time, Dante was a man of letters and wisdom, but above all a man of deep faith.

Through Dante we see, taste, feel, and touch the worlds of three afterlife planes: hell, purgatory, heaven. Images spring forth with such vivid imagery that the hereafter becomes palpable and ever so believable. In all three levels of the afterlife, angels are as real as earthly creatures.

As Dante swirls us around the depths of the Inferno, we feel in our bones the suffering of the condemned souls and the misery of life without God. As we hear the wails and moans of souls being cleansed in purgatory, angel multitudes provide hope and comfort. On the cornice of the greedy, you can almost hear the angelic choir sing the "Gloria" (Canto XX, 136).

To reacquaint myself with Dante and to soak up his verbal imagery, I decided to delve into *The Divine Comedy*. What a surprise awaited me! Instead of reading and imagining, I was drawn into a deep prayer experience. In company with Dante, Beatrice, and the saints in glory, I was wafted to the heavens. Prayer and contemplation came easy. I prayed as Dante: "O Divine Power, lend yourself to me, that I may discover a shadow of the beatific realm imprinted on my mind" (Canto I, 24, paraphrased).

As I strolled along the various levels of heaven, I was no longer a spectator, but a participant in the glories of the blessed. Joy and perfect peace gripped my imagination and emotions. I was so engrossed and drawn into the glory of heaven that I actually lost sight of my initial purpose. "I saw contained bound by love in one volume, what is scattered on separate pages throughout the world" (Canto XXXIII, 84).

As angels gracefully spiraled upward toward the Center of Divine Love, I was surrounded by the ethereal light and, like Dante, I felt myself embraced by a deep serenity which filled me with profound awe. The angels "like a swarm of bees descended into the white mystic rose pulsating…adorned with the petals of the blessed to the

center where divine love dwells" (Canto XXXI, 9, paraphrased).

Interestingly enough, my reverie turned into an ardent desire to commune more fully with the Lord as facilely as the blessed and the angels. I lifted my heart to God and entered the "still point," where I "unwintered" my soul and gave praise to God, just like the angels, according to Dante. I not only therein discovered God and the angels, but a deeper sense of myself and the dignity to which I am called to share with the angels.

No longer did heaven seem some sort of future mirage. Rather, I possessed heaven in the present moment as calm and peace swept over me. I prayed as did the apostles at the Transfiguration: "Lord, it is good for me to be here." Instinctively, Psalm 8 came to mind: "When I look at your heavens, the work of your fingers, / ...what are human beings that you are mindful of them?" I sang in my heart: "Yahweh I know you are near." Reluctantly I closed *The Divine Comedy* and returned to my mundane world on a spiritual high.

By reading Dante in prayerful reflection, I experienced in some small way the joy the angels possess. I befriended the saints and angels and felt communion with them, who behold the perfect love of the vision of God. I do not purport to be a mystic, but I know that by immersing myself into *The Divine Comedy* I was graced with a deeper rapport with the angels and a more ardent love of the Lord. Dante has truly enlightened me in a memorable encounter with the "lifestyles" of the blessed and angelic.

Conclusion

Dante is hailed as a literary genius for *The Divine Comedy*. He first titled the epic *Comedy* because it had a happy ending. The adjective "Divine" was added later due to its spiritual content.

Literature truly is the "power of the word" in its

transforming ability. The written word brings angels closer to us earthlings.

Music is another creative expression that intensely expresses the deep emotions of the human heart. Plato noted: "Music is to the mind as air is to the body." As a universal language of human feelings, music inspires beauty and is a fitting vehicle that can transport us into the world of the spirit, bringing us to the threshold of the Infinite. We associate music with angels because music puts our emotions in touch with angels and helps us sense their presence. Through music, we can feel a sublime serenity akin to the worshipful praise of the angels.

Music comes natural to angels. Throughout Scripture angels make melody, sing, dance, and play lutes, lyres, harps, timbrels, and clashing cymbals—all in praise of the Lord. Small wonder that we can easily feel at one with the angelic hosts through music's reverential piety, majestic splendor, or graceful tempos. Traditional Christian hymns are replete with angelic strains and references, suggesting perhaps that the angels sing with us in our worship and liturgical praise.

The great classical masters have produced music that emulates angelic harmony. The concertos, symphonies, and sonatas of Mendelssohn, Beethoven, Bach, Brahms, Mozart and others touch the human spirit. Classical masters who have produced majestic missa cantatas include Palestrina, Mozart, and Bach. For example, Bach's Mass in B Minor exemplifies angelic music par excellence.

"Ave Maria": Of special note is the "Ave Maria" set to music by the masters, especially Schubert, Gounod, and Liszt. As we listen to the inspiring chords, we cannot help but hear the angel Gabriel addressing the humble maid of Nazareth with the message that changed

human history. The "Ave Maria," as prayer, as music, and as both, is a perennial favorite of people of all faiths.

Gregorian chant: With its free-flowing rhythm, simplicity, and timelessness, Gregorian chant reechoes angel voices. The recent popularity of the album "Chant," by the Benedictine monks of Santo Domingo de Silos, attests to the perennial inspiration of plain song.

Oratorios: Sung by a chorus with full orchestra, recitations, solos, and interludes, an oratorio conveys dramatic devotion without props or scenery, thus heightening its ethereal impact. The most popular oratorio is George Frederick Handel's *Messiah*. Who is not moved by the majestic crescendo of the "Hallelujah Chorus": truly mystical experience in the company of the angels themselves!

Another oratorio that effectively portrays angelic harmony is Cardinal John Henry Newman's poem *Dream of Gerontius*, put into melody by English composer Edmund Elgar. This is the tale of a dying man, Gerontius, and the conversations he has with his guardian angel. *The Dream of Gerontius* has spellbound audiences since it first played in London in 1902. One critic reviewed it as "the closest thing to heaven."

Personal Inspiration and Reflection With Music

Although we do not all have the same preferences, music has a fluidity that makes it a unique experience. As a classical music aficionado, I have favorite pieces that waft my soul to angelic heights. The quiet chords of a soothing melody, or a splendid trumpeting triumphal, easily draw me into the company of angels. For me, music is an ideal prayer facilitator. It reminds me of the cartoon of a monk in a record shop asking for music to pray by.

The following list highlights selections that have wide appeal. These pieces are "music to pray by" at its best; they raise the soul to the angelic realm. Beethoven's

"Moonlight Sonata," which literally sends me to the empyrean heavens, heads the list of "Charlenian" favorites. Others include:

Liebestraume No. 3 in A Flat by Liszt
"Largo" from *New World Symphony* by Dvorak
The Pachebel Canon by Pachebel
"Evening Star" from *Tannhauser* by Wagner
"Clair De Lune" by Debussy
"Morning" from *Peer Gynt Suite* by Grieg
"Mattinata" by Leoncavolla
Jesu, Joy of Man's Desiring Chorale by Bach
"Theme from Finlandia" by Sibelius
Piano Concerto in B-Flat Minor by Tchaikovsky

In addition to these classics, the lyrics to "Whispering Hope" and "You'll Never Walk Alone" help many people remember the company they have in their ever-present guardian angel.

Conclusion

We would be remiss if we did not mention in our angelic art forms that which poignantly expresses the agility, lightness, speed, and elegance of angels themselves, in response to music. I was spellbound recently as I watched performers skate to the "Ave Maria." As the graceful forms in gossamer and flowing silks glided seemingly weightless on the ice, I sensed angelic freedom and could almost see angels' translucent figures in motion.

Conclusion

Yes, angels and humans have a common meeting ground—in the arts. Angels' presence may be imperceptible, but our senses have drawn them into our world and have raised us into theirs. No matter how sophisticated or technologically perfect we become, we will remain in contact with the celestial realm through art, literature, and music. As you become more aware of how art forms present angels, ponder the power of our human senses and imagination.

I end this chapter with a poetic challenge, an original expression: "Become Angel-Friendly Through the Arts":

Walk the world with open sense
And find God and angels' presence intense.
Look at art, feeble toil of human hands
And see there divinity reaching out to all lands.
Read of the world and of things unseen,
And sense in those words angelic creature serene.
Listen to exultant harmony on harp and strings,
And find there a meeting place with creatures beings.
Watch ballet and dance as graceful human forms,
Glide as angels, bereft of life's bitter storms.
And so, my friend, allow angels into your world.
Sense celestial joy in splendor unfurled,
Revealed through human imagination
        in creative ways,
Through art, literature, and harmonious lays.

PART IV

Angels in Prayer and Human Experiences

Angel of God, my guardian dear,
to whom [God's] love commits me here,
ever this day (night) be at my side,
to light and guard, to rule and guide. Amen

Prayer: Our Lifeline

Sightless, she approached me, guided by her walking stick. As she veered so as not to bump into me, I remarked, "My, your cane is really reliable." Giving the cane a pat, she noted with a smile, "This is my lifeline. I reach out where I cannot see, and just trust that Angie—that's my cane's name—will open the way and lead me along. Of course, caring folks like you also guide me."

That incident explains prayer: a lifeline; a reaching out in trust to what is unseen. We, too, reach out for the unseen—our God—through worship and private prayer. We believe we are also joined in love and grace by spiritual ties with the extended family of God—the communion of saints—and we trust in the guidance of the saints and angels.

When we say the Creed, especially the assertion that "we believe in the communion of saints," we acknowledge the basic belief that the angels and the saints in heaven, the souls in purgatory, and those of us on earth are bonded in a mutual rapport. Because angels and saints live in the presence of God, we believe they "have pull" with God. As a result, our prayers often invoke their aid and assistance. We believe that the angels and the saints are concerned about our welfare, and that we can depend on them to lead us closer to God.

In this chapter we explore ways we can include angels in our worship and personal spirituality and how angels at times make their presence felt in our lives.

Angels and the Liturgy

No other human activity enables us to share more intimately in the communion of saints than does our participation in the liturgy. We are invited to "lift up our hearts to the Lord," as we transcend to that world that is natural and indigenous to angels, the realm of the Divine. We are joined by the hosts of angels and saints in our worship of the Lord, who offers himself to the Father. "Countless hosts stand before you to do your will; they

look upon your splendor and praise you night and day" (Eucharistic Prayer IV).

During the liturgy, we offer to God the best we have to offer: the body and blood of his Son under the appearance of bread and wine. We join our voices with the hymn of the seraphim, "Holy, Holy, Holy." Angels surround the altar and worship Christ who has not only become man but also is present as the "bread of angels."

The sanctuary of the church is as the Holy of Holies— the earthly gathering of the heavenly hosts. If we keep this in mind, we can recapture a sense of the sacred amid the profane and so blend our earthly cares with the unbounded adoration of the angels. Gathered around the altar, our liturgy becomes more devout when we remember we are joined by a celestial entourage. As we pay attention to the liturgical prayers, we realize how often we pray "with all the angels and saints...."

To keep ourselves focused, we ask the angels to join us in our worship and to quiet our souls so we can be fully present and aware of the great mystery. After Communion we pray that the angels join us in praise of Christ who is fully and intimately present.

Angels and Our
Final Destiny

Our angel, who has been our constant companion during life, is most closely present to us at the hour of our death. We believe that our angel eases our passing by being most attentive to our welfare as we are about to leave this life. Numerous accounts of persons who have had near-death experiences attest to the calm and serenity they sensed in the presence of a peaceful light.

The Catholic Church celebrates the presence of angels in our lives and also at our death. At the Catholic funeral liturgy, the Church prays that the soul may be led into its heavenly reward accompanied by the angels.

The Roman ritual honors the archangels Michael, Gabriel, and Raphael with a liturgical feast on September 29. The guardian angels are honored on October 2 with an obligatory memorial, which supersedes optional or votive masses. A mass in honor of the angels can be celebrated on days when votive masses are allowed.

We believe that angels and saints are powerful intercessors for us in our human needs before God. Some saints are known to be more effective in certain causes, and have been named as "patron saints." Among those listed as "patron saints" are the three angels we honor in the Catholic Church.

Patrons

Michael: Michael, saint and angel, is the warrior who fends off the powers of evil. He is patron of policemen, seafarers, paratroopers, soldiers, knights, and is our overall protector against wicked forces. Michael is also the patron of grocers, possibly because he is pictured with the scales of justice. Why Michael is patron of radiologists is open to conjecture.

Gabriel: Gabriel, saint and angel, dispatches heavenly messages to earth. Understandably, he is the patron of communications media personnel, writers, telephone operators, and postal employees.

Raphael: As a healer and traveling companion, Raphael is patron of those in medical and pharmaceutical professions, travelers, and travel agents. Raphael is patron of the blind and those suffering from eye diseases because he instructed Tobias to apply fish gall to his father's eyes to restore his sight. Because Raphael was instrumental in bringing young Tobias and Sarah together, he is the patron of lovers and of happy reunions. Raphael is also the patron of sheep farmers, possibly because Tobit generously donated the first shearings of his sheep to the Lord (Tobit 1:6).

Spirituality and Devotion to Angels

As a child, I simply could not understand why human beings could not be in more than one place at a time. As I grew older and wiser, I realized that we can be present to others in a variety of ways. Prayer involves that same versatility. In our relationship with angels, we can use different methods of prayer. In the following section we consider diverse ways we can involve angels in our personal prayers and spirituality.

Spontaneous, Conversational Prayer

Spontaneous, conversational prayer is ordinary, simple small talk. It has no glitz, no frills. Because this kind of prayer is casual, our day provides a wealth of opportune moments—small pockets of time—for engaging in loving verbal exchanges with God and our guardian angel.

Because your angel is your constant companion along life's way, include your guardian angel in everyday life. Share your life's secrets and heartfelt desires with your angel. Be open to the wonder and comfort of your heavenly companion.

Traditional "Angel of God" Prayer

At times we may wish to pray with a set formula. Most of us raised as Catholics recall the "Prayer to Your Guardian Angel" that we learned as children. Because of its simple wisdom, the prayer is timeless; we never outgrow its gentle power. The "Angel of God" prayer has withstood the test of time and is useful in many life situations.

Angel of God, my guardian dear, to whom [God's] love commits me here, ever this day (night) be at my side, to light and guard, to rule and guide. Amen.

This short prayer can be learned by young children as an appropriate night prayer at the bedside. Because it focuses on protection, the prayer is also a beautiful way to begin a journey or fill those waiting times in the parking lot, at the railroad crossing, while waiting for the bus, or standing in line at the checkout counter. Because the "Angel of God" prayer is short and simple, even those who are very ill can find solace and comfort in reciting it.

Scripture is an excellent source for reflective meditation on angels. The Word of God portrays numerous ways angels aid us in our spiritual journey.

Meditation With Scripture

Select a favorite passage in which angels are mentioned. Read the passage slowly and try to put yourself in the event. Ask yourself, *How does this situation compare to my role and station in life? What can I glean spiritually by reflecting on this text?* Resolve to act on the inspiration you receive. You may be surprised to realize the powerful influence angels have in your life today.

One of my favorite Bible stories is about Jacob wrestling with the angel (Genesis 32:22-32). It reminds me of the times in my life when I balk at the will of God. Each time I reflect on this passage I am challenged to be more accepting and open to what the Lord is asking of me.

Much of the literature that has recently been written about angels deals with people's personal experiences of angels. This phenomena is a popular drawing card because we are a news-oriented society and like to read human interest accounts. The stories about persons who have angel experiences are inspirational and uplifting. The accounts help us to be more attuned to a greater power at work in our lives. These stories can heighten our awareness of how angels assist us toward a more intense spiritual life and deeper relationship with the Lord.

Reflective Reading

When reading these accounts, however, be wary of twisted theology. Although wondrous things may happen for which we have no explanation, angels cannot be manipulated to converse with us or cajoled to send messages from the beyond. All supernatural experiences are gratuitous gifts of God. As inspirational as they are, written accounts serve primarily as testaments to the glory and praise of the Lord.

Contemplation   If you think contemplation is reserved for mystics and saints, then the word itself may well intimidate you. Yet contemplation is part of our nature. We "contemplate" a project; we plan and "contemplate" a course of action; we "contemplate" the past; we "contemplate" the future; we "contemplate" significant decisions; we stand in "contemplation" before a spectacular sunset; we marvel at the wonder of life as we "contemplate" a sleeping infant.

Contemplation is necessary if we are to live life meaningfully and purposefully—and it contributes to a well-rounded life of prayer. Contemplation is the simplest of prayer forms: a wordless, loving resting in the Divine. It is quiet wonder and openness to the reality of the Spirit in our life. Praying is searching for and resting in God. But if God seems too grand, why not search out your angel?

To contemplate in the company of your angel, select a quiet time and place. In this time and place, put aside all your mundane concerns, and allow the love of your angel to encircle you. Imagine how your angel has great concern and care for you. In return, love your angel.

Sense the tranquillity and serenity of the moment, and allow your angel's love and energy to permeate your being. Sit silently in the presence of your angelic companion, and accept any inspiration that comes along. Only in contemplative quiet can God get through to a listening soul. You will return to your concerns renewed and rejuvenated.

Contemplative Centering Prayer   If you have difficulty settling into quiet, if you find wordless contemplation not to be your prayer style, if your mind flits from one thought to another like a restless butterfly, consider using one word. Think of an angelic trait you wish to imbibe into your being. Then, repeat the word slowly as you take in each breath, peace or joy or serenity, for example. After a period of time, you can return to your daily routine refreshed and more aware of your angel's presence in your life.

Besides through prayer, we can also experience the presence of angels by mirroring their ways: by spontaneous acts of kindness and goodness. The highest compliment we can receive is "You're such an angel!"

Be an Angel

Fortunately, we need not wait for an official random-acts-of-kindness day to display angelic goodness. We can make every day special and thus intensify and make visible angels' presence through our virtuous angel-like actions.

In India, persons greet each other with folded hands, a reverential bow, and a greeting such as, "Namaste," which translates as "I greet the Divine in you." We can imitate this practice with a benevolent look as we greet others and their angels present with them.

Angels are not merely theological conclusions or abstract realities; angels are created, active beings in touch with our world and interested in our human activities. The world is, in fact, embraced by angelic beings who lovingly guide and inspire us. It is understandable that these beings, graced by God, have a vested concern in humankind: we are destined to share divine life with them.

Angels in Human Experience

Catholic doctrine teaches that the angels are involved in our affairs and that, at times, God graces certain individuals with "proof" of their presence. The lives of the saints are filled with examples of those who have tangible experiences of angels. Francis of Assisi, for example, was gifted with the stigmata, the wounds of Christ, by a seraphim. Frances of Rome, a widow and mystic, and Gemma Galgani, a household servant, felt and saw the presence of their angels in their daily lives. Joan of Arc, summoned by archangel Michael, led the

French army to victory over the English. Such angel encounters, fortunately, are not relegated to the mystics and the saints of the Middle Ages. Today's angel encounters continue to inspire us to awe.

It seems we are more attuned to the Divine as we pay more attention to angelic presences. Each person's experience of an angel's presence is a unique, never-to-be-repeated event.

In preparation for this work, I talked to a lot of people about angels. Almost everyone shared an angel story. They recounted experiences ranging from a subtle peaceful feeling to intense feelings which hint of the mystical.

Consolation in prayer: The most subtle spiritual experience can come when we are engrossed in prayer. We may be pouring out our soul to the Lord, when a peaceful calm enfolds us and we sense a spiritual presence, which possibly may be our angel. Often this serenity and peace occurs when we are open to the graces of the Lord.

Coincidental happenings: Sometimes we make a decision for no specific reason, only to find that the decision prevented us from being involved in some mishap. We may call this a premonition, coincidence, or intuitive hunch, and may not attribute it to angelic intervention in the moment. In hindsight, however, when all other reasons fail, we begin to ponder the possibility of angelic intervention. Although angels cannot foresee the future, they are higher intelligences and can sense the imminence of impending danger.

Those who have gone through this experience affirm that it was more than a hunch or a coincidence. Most people who tell of an extraordinary intervention believe it was supernatural, and are firm in believing its truth.

Angel Encounters   The most popular accounts written about angel encounters concern people who have been miraculously

74

helped in a drastic situation by a "stranger" who disappears as fast as he/she appears. Those who attest to such mysterious visits affirm they have been helped by an angel. The experience leaves them in awe, changed for the better, and staunchly believing in angels. Those of us who listen to their accounts owe respect to the experience. Recall the biblical caution, "Do not neglect to show hospitality to strangers, for by doing that some have entertained angels without knowing it" (Hebrews 13:2).

These occurrences belong to the realm of individual experience and are graced events for an individual. God does manifest his divine plan to us in myriads of ways.

Apparitions and Visions

The most unusual and intense spiritual experience occurs when we become totally absorbed into the spiritual realm. The moment may be experienced as a vision of light or of an ethereal being robed in white. We feel oneness and unity with all of creation, while enjoying the grasp of a higher power that is friendly and peaceful. The experience is transitory and leaves us in wonder and awe. We cannot program ourselves for such an experience, as it is a totally gratuitous grace of the Lord.

People who have had near-death experiences speak of seeing radiant, subtle auras of light or a figure that exudes compassion, kindness, and peaceful harmony. Although such experiences are not commonplace, we must be wary of dismissing them. The evidence is subjective and depends entirely on the sincerity and credibility of the beholder.

Remarkable tales of angel visitations may leave us shaking our heads in awe. An authentic angel encounter always makes us a better person and leads us closer to the Lord, which is the very essence of religious experiences. Such encounters help us preserve our sense of wonder, bolster our faith in supernatural protection and guidance, and reinforce our awareness of God at work in the world.

Conclusion   While our world is riddled with violence, crime, and grief brought on by our brokenness and sinfulness, faith abides in our midst, for there, too, is justice, love, and peace. In this world where evil continues to roam, angels represent all that is noble, holy, and pure. As human beings, we yearn for that kind of world in which peace, happiness, and joy may be ours. Angels remind us that it is possible.

Let us rejoice in the aura of the angelic goodness and innocence that encircles our earth. Let us pattern our lives on angelic traits, and thus enhance human life. Let us escalate our efforts to bring goodness within and around this fragile but divinely favored planet in God's vast universe. For while the interest in angels may be a sign of increased spiritual awareness, it remains obvious that angels are, indeed, with us. If their presence makes a difference, if only to a few, let us welcome them with open arms.

Angels are not a new phenomenon, but an ageless mystery of faith that has been with us throughout the ages. Let us welcome into our spirituality the angelic world resurrected and revitalized. We praise and thank God for his wisdom in creating these beings of peace and goodness. May we all realize the angels' steady guidance, feel their power, and sense the calm and silent world of the Spirit. May we travel our journey of faith with the awareness of being invisibly companioned by our own angel, who brings comfort and solace to us along life's way.

I do not walk alone! How awesome!
Invisibly companioned along life's treacherous way
By you: a being of goodness and gentleness.
A deep mystery too wonderful for my myopic view!
My fragile being cannot withstand
Your august majesty, O celestial friend.

Mediator with God on my behalf,
Nudge me along gently;
Envelop me with kindness,
Gentleness, and sweet ways.
Let fear not overtake the goodness
I long to portray.

Friend of my soul,
Smile at my gawkiness,
And join in my moments of joy and elation.
Console and enfold me in your caring embrace,
Especially in those times when I need to know
I am not fighting my earthly battle alone.

Angel of light, inspiration,
Loving presence, constant guide,
I am humbled to realize
That I have you with me—always—
My steady companion, my guardian angel.

Graced by God with superior intelligence,
You stand in the presence of the Almighty.
I join you in praising God for your existence.

O angel most pure, how sad you must be,
When I swerve from the path of doing good
And give in to my baser drives.
Little do I realize that when I think
My insights are my own,
It is really you, O angel, who is inspiring me.

If ever I forget you, blessed companion,
Alert me to your presence with tenderness and
      love.
Be to me a guide, a companion, a true guardian,
The one who understands my fickle human ways.

Amen.

About the Author

Sister Charlene Altemose, MSC, is a Missionary Sister of the Most Sacred Heart (Reading, Pennsylvania) with degrees in education, theology, and journalism. Her ministries have included teaching college theology, writing newspaper columns and articles, directing parish adult education, and being active in interfaith activities and the Council of Churches.

Sister Charlene was awarded a Fulbright scholarship to India and a Christian Leadership grant to Israel. As a result of her scholarship excellence, she was invited to be a presenter at the 1993 Council for a Parliament of World Religions.

Author of *Why Do Catholics...?* (Brown-Roa), and *What You Should Know About the Mass, What You Should Know About the Catechism of the Catholic Church,* and *What You Should Know About the Sacraments* (Liguori), Sister Charlene also conducts workshops, retreats, and adult education programs.